Helping Hands

At the Dentist

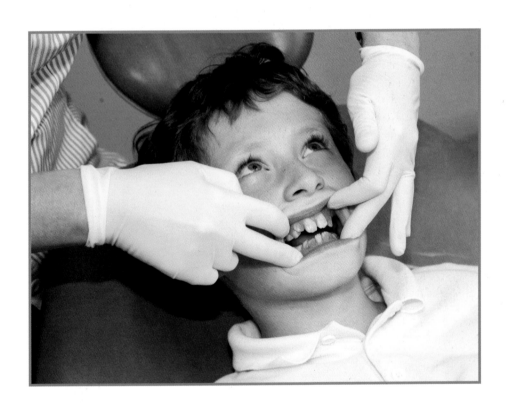

Chris Fairclough and Louise Morrish

WAYLAND

First published in 2008 by Wayland

Copyright © Wayland 2008

Wayland,
Hachette Children's Books
338 Euston Road
London NW1 3BH

Wayland Australia
Hachette Children's Books
Level 17/207 Kent Street
Sydney, NSW 2000

Managing Editor: Rasha Elsaeed
Editor: Katie Powell
Design: Ruth Cowan
Commissioned photography: Chris Fairclough

British Library Cataloguing in Publication Data:

Fairclough, Chris
   At the dental surgery. - (Helping hands)
   1. Dental personnel - Juvenile literature
   I. Title
   617.6'023

ISBN 978 0 7502 5244 7

Printed and bound in China

Wayland is a division of Hachette Children's Books, an
Hachette Livre UK company.

Acknowledgements
The author and publisher would like to thank the staff and
patients at King Street Dental Practice in Odiham, Hampshire
for their help and participation in this book.

The website addresses (URLs) included in this book were
valid at the time of going to press. However, because of the
nature of the Internet, it is possible that some addresses may
have changed, or sites may have changed or closed down
since publication. While the author and Publisher regret any
inconvenience this may cause the readers, no responsibility
for any such changes can be accepted by either the author
or the Publisher.

Contents

Words printed in **bold** are explained in the glossary.

The team

We work at a dental **surgery**. Dentists and a team of people look after a **patient's** teeth. The office staff help to organise the surgery and make sure it runs well.

We are a team of five dentists, six dental nurses, two **hygienists**, three **receptionists** and a practice manager. ▼

The surgery has a **reception**, waiting room and treatment rooms where patients go to have their teeth checked.

▲ We work in an old building that has been turned into a dental surgery.

We have plenty of magazines and toys for patients to use while they wait. ▼

The reception

When patients first arrive at the dental surgery, they see a receptionist. Receptionists do all kinds of different jobs.

◄ We greet patients and tell them which dentist they will be seeing.

I am making an **appointment** for a patient who is phoning the surgery. We send out reminder cards to patients at home. ▶

A practice manager makes sure the dental surgery runs smoothly.

▲ I'm the practice manager and I look after the surgery building and the people who work here.

This patient has just finished seeing the dentist and has come back to the reception to pay. ▼

The dentist

A dentist is a doctor who looks after teeth. Every six months dentists check to see if a patient has any teeth or gum problems. They repair damaged or **decaying** teeth.

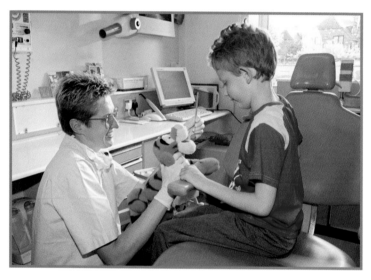

▲ I use this tiger to show Luke how I will check his teeth and gums.

Luke sits in a big chair. It has a rest for his head, a bright light to see inside his mouth and a sink so he can rinse his mouth. ▶

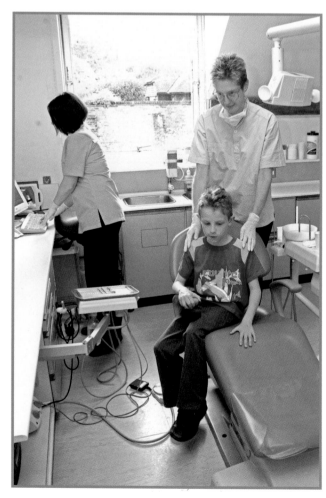

If a tooth is broken or chipped a dentist can rebuild it. Dentists also treat gum disease, such as **gingivitis**.

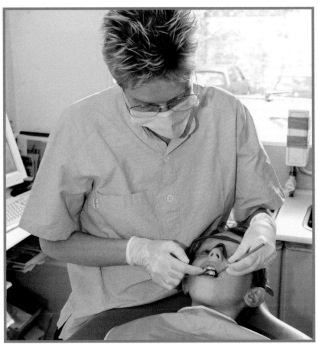

▲ I then check each of Luke's teeth. If he needs treatment then we make an appointment for him to come back.

After I have finished Luke's check-up, I let him choose a sticker to show he has been a good patient. ▶

RINGSEND BRANCH TEL. 6680063

The dental nurses

Dental nurses help the dentists. They wear special tunics to protect their clothes and a mask and gloves to prevent the spread of infection.

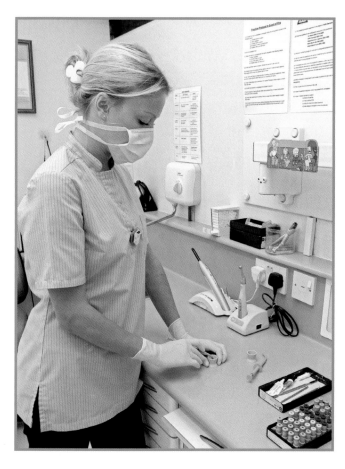

▲ I am preparing the mixture used for a **filling**.

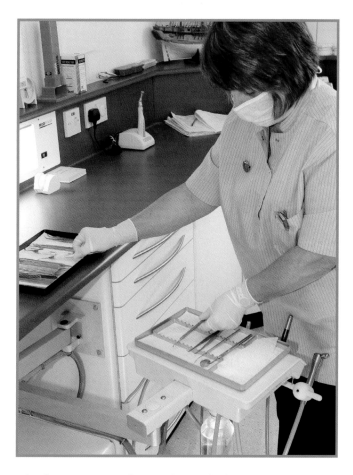

▲ I am getting the right dental tools and equipment ready for the dentist.

Nurses make sure that the surgery is kept clean and they help the dentists to prepare their **equipment**.

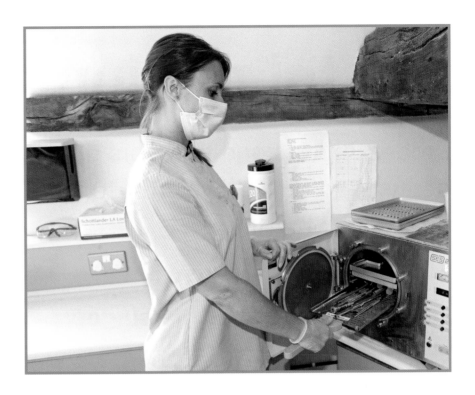

▲ All the equipment has to be **sterilised**. We use a machine called an autoclave to do this.

I am checking a patient's **dental records** on the computer with the dentist. ▼

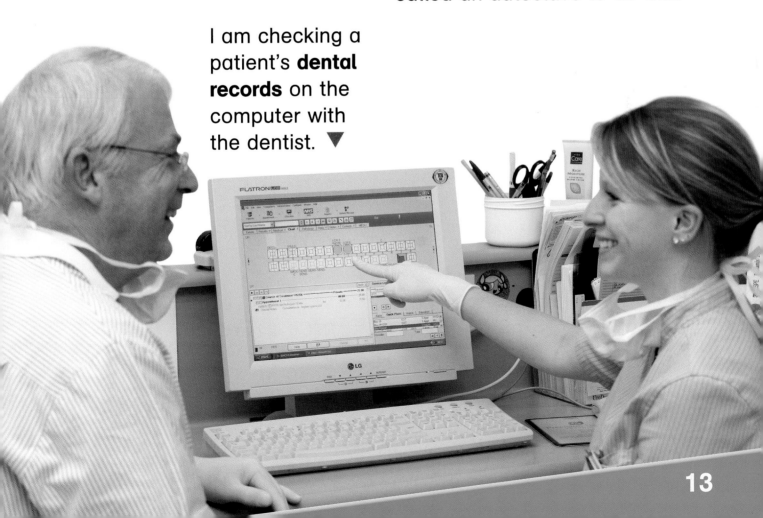

Dental equipment

Probes, mirrors and tweezers all help the dentist and dental hygienist to check, repair and clean your teeth.

Dental equipment at the surgery

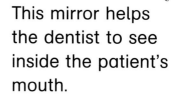

This mirror helps the dentist to see inside the patient's mouth.

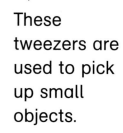

These tweezers are used to pick up small objects.

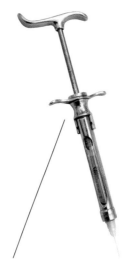

This syringe is used for giving **injections**.

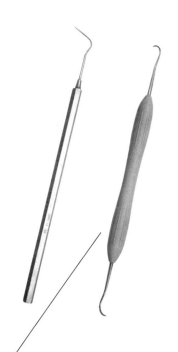

These two probes help the dentist check teeth for decay.

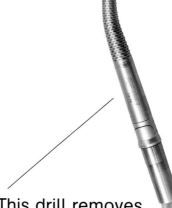

This drill removes soft decay from the tooth.

These cotton wool rolls keep the mouth dry.

Dental equipment at home

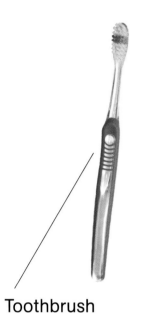

Toothbrush

Toothbrush head that attaches to an electric toothbrush.

New electric toothbrush head

Electric toothbrush and charger.

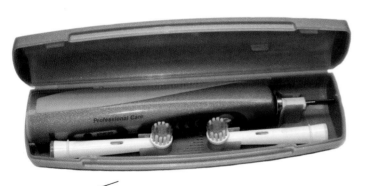

Case to carry electrical toothbrush.

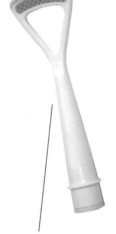

Dental floss is used to clean in between teeth.

The tongue freshner attaches to the electric toothbrush and is used to scrape the tongue.

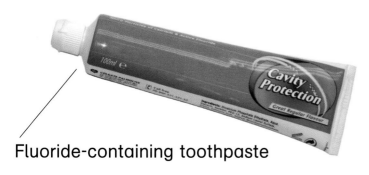

Fluoride-containing toothpaste

X-rays

Dentists use **X-ray** machines to help them see what is happening to our teeth and gums. They use them to plan our treatment.

I am taking an X-ray of Toby's teeth. I make sure the X-ray machine is in the right place. Toby bites into a piece of X-ray film. ▶

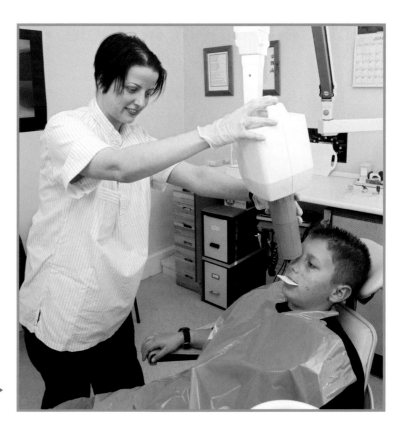

◀ Then I stand back and press the button. The X-ray machine doesn't hurt Toby. In fact, he doesn't feel a thing!

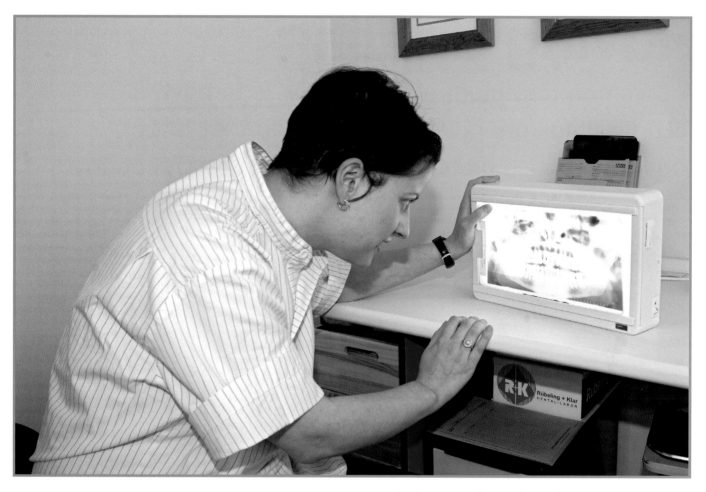

▲ I examine the X-ray of Toby's teeth. He may need a filling removed.

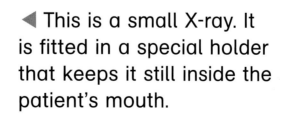

◀ This is a small X-ray. It is fitted in a special holder that keeps it still inside the patient's mouth.

Having a filling

A common treatment at the dentist is to have a filling. Fillings are caused by bacteria that attack teeth and cause **plaque**. This makes the tooth decay.

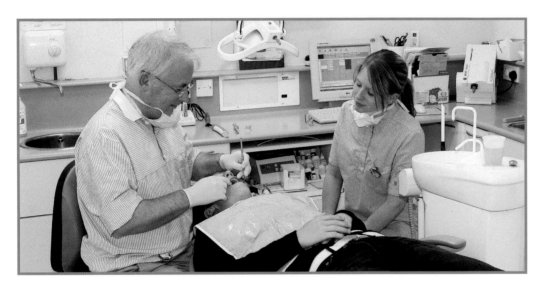

◀ I'm the dentist and I'm looking inside Josh's mouth.

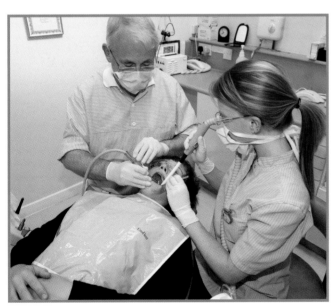

▲ I can see one of Josh's teeth has a small **cavity** and needs a filling.

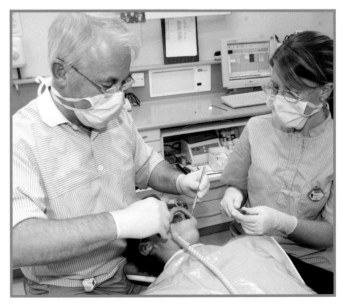

▲ I clean out the inside of the tooth with a water drill. This gets rid of the decay and leaves a small hole in the tooth.

I fill the hole with a soft filling mixture. Then I use a light cure machine to set the filling. This hardens the filling mixture. ▶

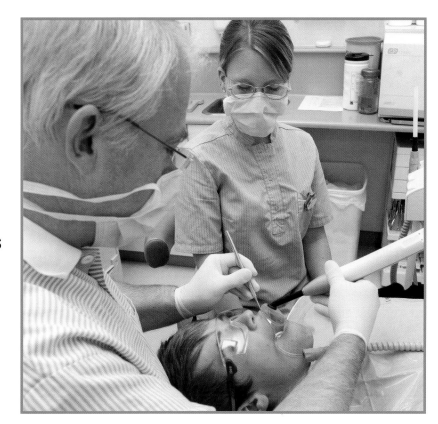

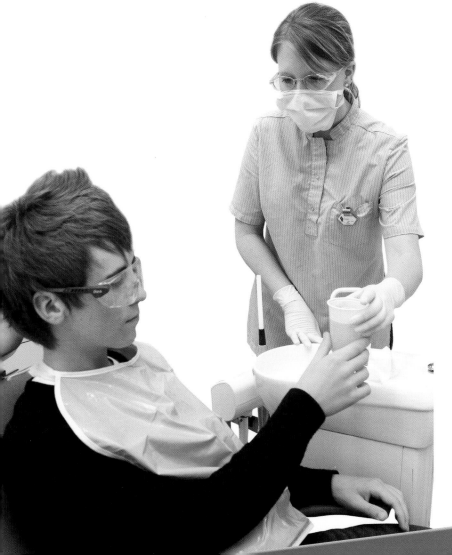

◀ I'm the dental nurse. When the dentist has finished, I help Josh to rinse his mouth out with an **antiseptic mouthwash**.

Special treatment

If a dentist cannot repair a tooth then it may have to be removed. Teeth may also need to be straightened with a brace or a crown may need to be fitted to a chipped tooth.

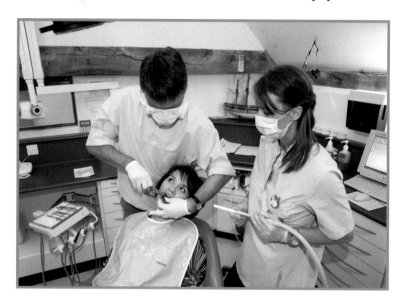

◄ Sarah has had an **anaesthetic** to numb her mouth. This prevents any pain when the dentist removes her tooth.

Braces are used to straighten crooked teeth. I am adjusting this patient's braces so they fit. ▶

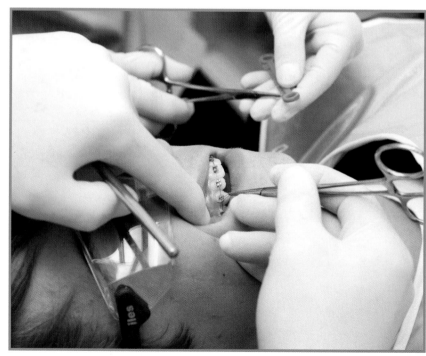

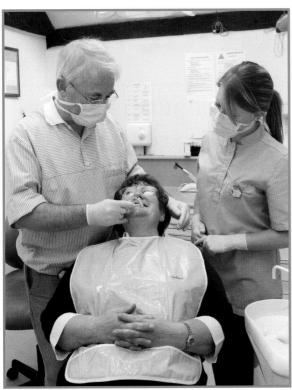

◀ This patient is having **dentures** fitted.

If a patient is too sick to come to the surgery, the dentist will visit them at home. ▶

Emergency treatment

In an emergency, people need to see a dentist straight away. Maybe a tooth has broken or it is very painful and needs to come out.

Alex's tooth was knocked out while he was playing in a football match. ▶

◀ Alex puts his tooth in a glass of milk to help keep it alive.

◀ His friend Ross takes him to the dental surgery for emergency treatment.

Alex goes to the dentist to have his tooth replaced. The dentist can put the tooth back into Alex's mouth but this needs to be done within one hour of the tooth falling out for the gum to tighten up and heal.

I am wearing glasses called magnifying loupes. They make things look bigger and help me to see the damage in Alex's mouth more clearly. ▼

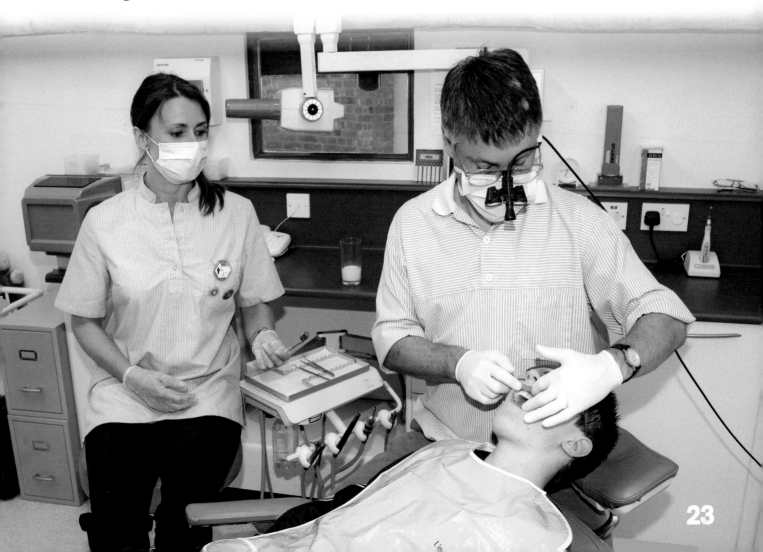

Dental hygienists

Dental hygienists clean, scrape and polish teeth. They use dental floss to get in between the teeth.

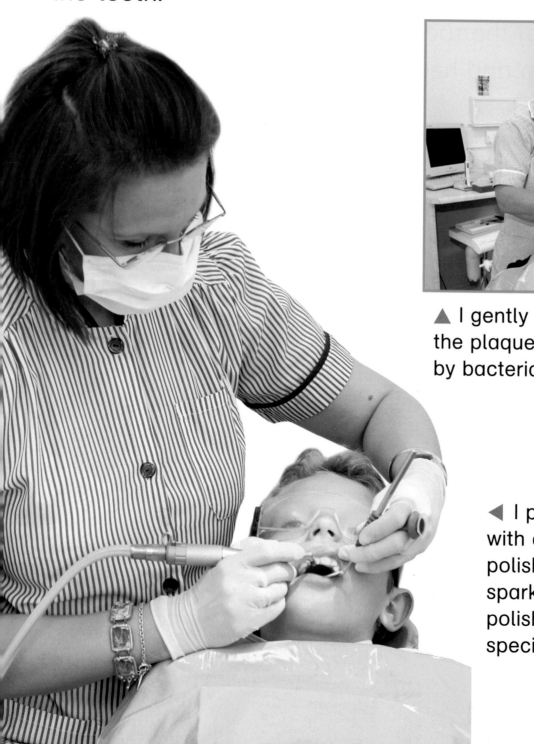

▲ I gently scrape away the plaque which is caused by bacteria.

◀ I polish Luke's teeth with an electric polisher so that they sparkle! I keep the polishing paste in my special ring.

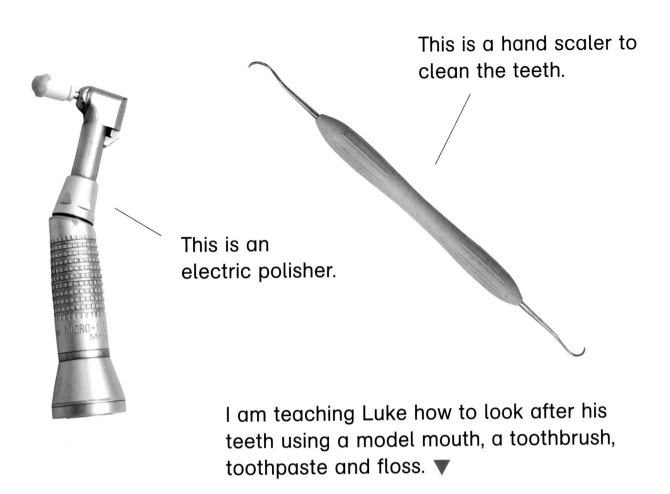

This is a hand scaler to clean the teeth.

This is an electric polisher.

I am teaching Luke how to look after his teeth using a model mouth, a toothbrush, toothpaste and floss. ▼

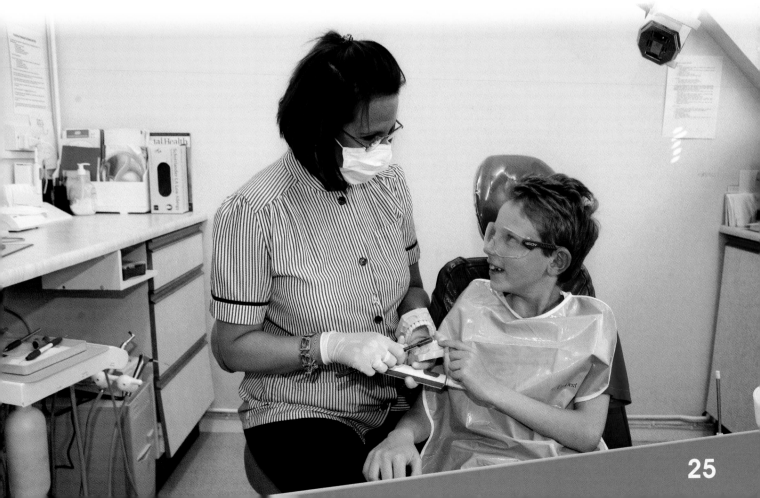

Healthy teeth

Everyone should go to the dentist for a check-up once every six months. We need to brush our teeth twice a day for two minutes to keep our teeth and gums clean and healthy.

We sell toothbrushes at the dental surgery. Children should replace their toothbrushes every six weeks. ▼

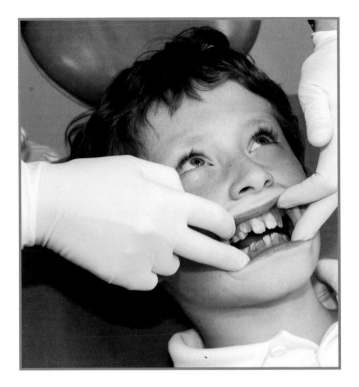

◀ Lewis has chewed a **disclosing tablet.** Where there is still plaque on his teeth, they turn pink. This helps me to see if Lewis has been cleaning his teeth properly!

Disclosing tablets

How to keep your teeth and gums healthy

✳ Visit the dentist every six months.

✳ Replace your toothbrush every six weeks.

✳ Use a flouride toothpaste.

✳ Eat lots of fruit and vegetables.

✳ Drink lots of milk.

✳ Avoid too many sugary snacks and drinks.

✳ Clean your teeth twice a day, after breakfast and before you go to bed.

✳ Brush all of your teeth, not just the front ones.

✳ Make sure you floss your teeth.

Glossary

anaesthetic a substance that makes a tooth go numb

antiseptic mouthwash a liquid that you rinse round your mouth to kill germs

appointment a time when a dentist arranges to see a patient

cavity a decayed part of a tooth

decay the rotten part of a tooth

dental record notes that contain details of a patient

dentures a set of false teeth

disclosing tablet a tablet that colours parts of the teeth that haven't been cleaned properly

equipment the tools people use to do their job

filling a small piece of material put inside a cavity to fill the hole in a decayed tooth

gingivitis a gum disease where the gums around the teeth become red and swollen and can bleed when brushed

hygienist someone who is trained to clean teeth

injection a way of giving anaesthetic or medicine using a syringe

patient a person who is looked after by a dentist or nurse

plaque a soft layer that forms on the teeth in between brushing. It can cause tooth decay and gum disease

reception the place where patients check-in for their appointment

receptionist a person who works at a reception

sterilise to clean something and kill germs using heat or steam

surgery the place where dentists or doctors see patients

syringe a small cylinder with a needle attached. It is used for injections

X-ray a photograph that shows bones. Dentists use X-rays to see what is happening inside teeth and gums.

Quiz

Look back through the book to do this quiz.

1 How often should you visit the dentist for a check-up?

2 What is the machine that sterilises the dentist's equipment called?

3 Why do dentists use X-ray machines?

4 What does a dental hygienist do?

5 How often should you change your toothbrush?

6 How long should you brush your teeth for, and how many times a day?

7 What do disclosing tablets show?

Answers

1 Every six months.

2 An autoclave.

3 To see inside people's teeth and gums.

4 Cleans and polishes teeth.

5 Every six weeks.

6 For two minutes, twice a day.

7 If your teeth have been cleaned properly.

Useful contacts

www.kidshealth.org/kid/stay_healthy /body/teeth.html
Covers how the body works and describes why teeth are important and how to take care of them.

www.healthyteeth.org
What goes on inside your mouth, produced by dentists with primary-school-aged children.

www.bbc.co.uk/schools/scienceclips /ages/6_7/health_growth_whatnext.s html
Games and quizzes about teeth in humans and animals.

Looking forward to seeing you at the surgery soon!

Index